10 Awesome Betta Fish Toys & Decorations to Help Beat Boredom...2

   Why Do I Need Toys for My Betta Fish?...............3

   Our Favorite Betta Fish Toys & Decorations 6

   Conclusion..24

BONUS 25

Marimo Moss Ball Care: The Compete Guide 26

   What is a Marimo Moss Ball? 27

   Why Do They Cost So Much?...............................28

   Marimo Moss Ball Care 30

   Common Uses of Marimo Moss Balls..................36

   Tank Mates...37

   Pros and Cons of Marimo Moss Balls 38

   Signs that your Moss Ball is Dying......................42

   How to Propagate your Moss Ball......................44

   Size..45

10 AWESOME BETTA FISH TOYS & DECORATIONS TO HELP BEAT BOREDOM

If you just got your first Betta fish, you may be wondering if your new friend is bored.

Bettas can't be kept with members of their own species due to their aggressive nature, leaving many aquarists to ponder getting theirs a few toys to keep him or her occupied.

Do Bettas need toys? Do they even like them? And if so, what are the best Betta fish toys?

Keep reading this Betta fish toy guide for the answers to these questions and more!

WHY DO I NEED TOYS FOR MY BETTA FISH?

Adding toys to your Betta's aquarium is actually an important part of Betta care – depending on your definition of toys, that is.

Although fish like Bettas don't tend to play with toys like a dog or a cat would, they need and appreciate them. There are three reasons for this.

1. TOYS HELP YOUR BETTA FISH BEAT BOREDOM

First off, in their natural habitat, a Betta will tend to have several square meters of territory to explore. This territory is generally patrolled diligently, as you'll likely also see your fish do in its tank.

Bettas spend much of their day swimming laps around the tank, keeping a close eye on all elements and checking out anything new.

Adding toys like a moss ball or some live plants changes things up and offers mental stimulation.

2. DECORATIONS HELP YOU BETTA FISH FEEL MORE CONFORTABLE

Additionally, Betta fish are naturally quite shy.

The ponds and swamps their wild counterparts naturally inhabit contain a LOT of vegetation, sometimes so much you wouldn't even think there was any water or fish present.

They're used to having all these plants to use as cover and therefore really appreciate plenty of hides. Many Betta fish toys are designed to not just provide mental stimulation, but also a hiding spot for your fish.

Don't worry about never seeing your Betta: having more hides reduces stress and will actually make the Betta more likely to stay out in the open, since it knows it can retreat at any time.

3. THEY GIVE YOU BETTA FISH PLACES TO RELAX

Third, Bettas, and especially long-finned varieties, really like having access to some resting spots.

Dragging around a broad tail that's just as long as its body itself is rather exhausting for the fish, especially because it needs to regularly dart to the surface to catch a breath of air.

To make things easier for your Betta you can add some of the many toys to its tank that are designed to double as resting places. Even a large-leaved plant that stretches up to the surface can be used as a fish sofa!

So, now that we've confirmed that your Betta does indeed appreciate and even need some toys in its tank for various reasons, let's move on and see what we've got to work with.

There are many natural and artificial types of Betta fish toys out there, so it shouldn't be difficult to find something that matches your aquarium set-up.

OUR FAVORITE BETTA FISH TOYS & DECORATIONS

Here are a few toys and accessories that your betta fish is sure to love!

PLANTS

The most common 'toy' to add to a Betta tank is really not a toy at all, but rather something natural and simple: live plants.

Greenery in the form of aquatic plants offers all of the advantages of Betta fish toys that we discussed earlier and will really be appreciated.

You don't have to go easy on the planting either, because the more jungle-like its tank, the more your Betta will like it.

If you've had bad experiences with live (aquarium) plants, you might be worried your black thumb will get in the way of successfully growing them in your tank.

An alternative to live plants exists in the form of artificial ones made of plastic and silk. These work absolutely fine and your Betta won't be able to tell the difference.

Just make sure any artificial plants you use are absolutely free of sharp edges that might tear a Betta's delicate fins.

Even if you haven't had much luck with growing plants in the past, we do still recommend at least considering it now.

Live plants offer additional benefits that artificial ones don't, like aiding in keeping the aquarium's water values stable by absorbing harmful substances such as nitrates.

There are many plant species out there that will thrive in your aquarium, some of which grow so prolifically even an absolute beginner will be able to keep them alive.

LEAF HAMMOCKS

Zoo Med Laboratories AZMBL20 Betta Hammock

- A naturalistic leaf hammock for your Betta to rest...
- The perfect resting hammock for your natural look...
- Attach near the top of your Betta's tank using the...

$4.86

[Buy on Amazon](#)

The Betta fish leaf hammock was designed focusing on the fact that Bettas need resting spots to feel comfortable.

This toy is as simple as it is ingenious: a broad plastic leaf invites your Betta to 'take a seat', while a suction cup allows you to place the leaf anywhere you'd like.

Near the surface is usually the best option, since most other décor doesn't stretch that high and your Betta will like not having to travel too far for a gulp of air.

There are various brands of Betta fish leaf hammocks out there, some of better quality than others.

You can't usually test the leaf hammock since they come pre-packaged, but try to inspect it for any sharp edges and try to go for a brand that is more silky rather than hard plastic.

BETTA FISH MIRRORS

One of the most commonly sold Betta fish toys is the classic mirror.

Bettas, having been bred as fighter fish, will respond very strongly to their own reflection.

Seeing themselves triggers a flaring reaction, where the fish expands its fins and gill flaps and takes on a threatening posture in order to scare off the 'opponent'.

Seeing your Betta flare is quite fascinating, but be careful not to overuse your Betta fish mirror. Definitely don't leave it in the tank indefinitely: being exposed to what it thinks is an opponent threatening its territory 24/7 is extremely stressful to a Betta.

Stress makes fish vulnerable to disease and other issues, so don't use a Betta fish mirror for more than five minutes a day.

You might be asking yourself why, if seeing its reflection stresses a Betta out, you'd use a Betta fish mirror at all?

In an aquarium a Betta doesn't get as much exercise as it would in a natural environment, which is one of the reasons this species is actually quite prone to obesity.

Making yours exercise for a few minutes a day won't stress it out and can help keep it a little bit healthier than it would otherwise be!

TRAINING KITS

R2 Fish School Complete Fish Training Kit

- Includes a 45 minute detailed instructional DVD...
- Includes a Full Color manual with over 100 photos...
- The easy to use, targeted feeding wand comes with...

$34.99

[Buy on Amazon](#)

If you're looking for a way to really interact with your Betta, the Fish School Training Kit might be the best toy to choose here.

This product is exactly what its name suggests: a kit that contains various different ways to train your Betta, teaching it to do tricks.

There's a hoop, a miniature football field and little balls for the fish to push around.

A small feeding wand that can hold a food pellet allows you to train the fish to perform the tricks included.

Users of this training kit have reported varying degrees of success with Bettas, with some of them seemingly being more motivated to chase a pellet around than others.

That being said, this is such a fun thing to try and some fish do appear to learn quickly!

CAVES

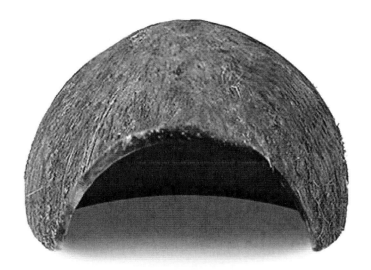

Coco Hut for Pets

Buy on Amazon

There are many different brands and shapes of caves out there that you can add to your aquarium décor. All serve the same basic purpose, though: helping your fish feel safe by offering it a spot to retreat to in case it feels threatened.

As we discussed earlier Betta fish are among the shyer aquarium fish species out there, so adding one or multiple cave-like structures to your tank is definitely helpful in keeping your Betta's stress levels down.

When choosing a cave for your Betta, be sure to inspect it thoroughly before placing it in the tank. All décor should lack sharp edges that your fish can hurt itself on.

Anything with holes small enough for a Betta to get stuck in should also be avoided. Additionally, try to find a cave that has at least two holes so water can freely flow in and out.

Caves with only one hole can become a place for water to become stagnant and rot, which can end up fouling your entire tank and endangering the health of your fish once the cave is disturbed.

HOOPS

The Fish School Training Kit we discussed before contains various elements that you can teach your Betta, including a hoop.

It seems that Betta owners have had most success with training their Betta to swim (or even jump!) through the hoop, as opposed to the other tricks.

If you don't want to break the bank by buying an entire training kit for your Betta, there are also a few brands out there that sell individual hoop kits.

As discussed earlier Bettas are prone to obesity due to inactivity and small aquarium environments, so making yours work for its food by jumping or swimming around is a great option to help keep it healthy.

MARIMO MOSS BALLS

Marimo Moss Ball

We've already discussed live plants and their advantages, but there is one 'plant' in particular that is so popular among Betta keepers it deserves its own spot on a list of Betta fish toys.

Actually consisting of a type of algae rather than moss, Marimo balls are very easy to care for and don't require a green thumb at all.

Your Betta will appreciate having one or multiple Marimo balls in its aquarium just as much as any other plant.

The moss balls offer a place to rest on and hide behind, as well as the added advantage of absorbing nitrates and thereby helping to keep your aquarium healthy.

One point to keep in mind about Marimo balls is that they naturally occur in lakes in cold areas, and although they are very adaptable when it comes to temperature you might want to avoid them if you keep your Betta tank at the upper end of the temperature range.

BETTA FISH BALLS

Because real Marimo moss balls don't always do well in higher temperatures, you might have to come up with another solution if your Betta tank seems to be a little too toasty for these algae to thrive.

Luckily there are some other spherical Betta toy options that work just as well!

The easiest Betta fish ball option that's not an actual moss ball would simply be a faux moss ball. Although these don't come with the added advantages that live plants offer, they do still help your fish feel safer and comfortable, as well as adding an extra element to its environment for it to explore.

If you do want something that is live like a Marimo ball, you can also opt to make your own moss ball using Java moss.

This hardy aquatic moss is much less sensitive to high temperatures and can be grown in a round shape using a moss dome.

For a floating option that your Betta can chase and that adds shelter at the water surface, a golf ball suffices just fine.

FLOATING LOGS

If you feel your Betta tank might be lacking hiding or resting spots near the surface, one great option is to add a floating Betta fish log.

This tubular ornament resembles a hollow floating log of wood, making for a natural look in the aquarium. It offers your fish a place to dart into when it feels threatened and also makes for a great sleeping spot, since it floats near the surface.

This makes it easier for the fish to take gulps of air, which a Betta needs to be able to do regularly as it has evolved to take up oxygen not just from water, but also from the air.

There are also sinking Betta fish logs, although those probably fall more into the cave category.

Adding one of both to your aquarium décor would be a great way to make sure your fish feels safe at any given moment.

INDIAN ALMOND LEAVES

Sale

SunGrow Indian Almond Leaves for Betta, 8 Inches Long, Induce Breeding and Boost Immunity, Reduce...

- ✔ INDUCE BREEDING --- SunGrow Betta Leaves are a...

- ✔ STRESS RELIEVER --- Bettas have been known to...
- ✔ FOR PLAYING AND HIDING --- Small shrimps, fry...

$18.95 –$1.51 $17.44

[Buy on Amazon](#)

If you have never used Indian Almond Leaves in your aquarium, you're seriously missing out!

Not only do these leaves give you tank a nice, natural look, but they also have tons of benefits as well.

Indian Almond Leaves are are known to reduce stress, add helpful minerals/elements back into the water, and boost the immune system of Bettas.

In addition, they are extremely simple to use – just drop a few into your tank and you (and your Betta) are good to go!

CONCLUSION

Although your Betta fish doesn't require toys to play with in the sense that a human would, it does need enrichment.

Luckily, as this list has hopefully illustrated, there are plenty of options out there to provide your Betta with what it needs to feel safe, well-rested and entertained!

A well-decorated aquarium that contains plenty of toys reduces the chances of your Betta becoming overweight and suffering from health problems like fatty liver disease, so choose your favorites and get to furnishing that tank.

BONUS

MARIMO MOSS BALL CARE: THE COMPETE GUIDE

Marimo (Aegagropila linnaei)

Marimo moss balls have been growing in popularity in the aquarium hobby.

But what exactly are these small green blobs, and what is so appealing about them?

This guides dives into everything you need to know about the Marimo moss ball, including care tips, optimal water parameters, tank mates, propagation, and more!

WHAT IS A MARIMO MOSS BALL?

While a Marimo moss ball looks like a small green plant, or maybe a moss, it is actually a spherical form of algae. In fact, "marimo" is a Japanese term that roughly translates to "algae ball".

While many circular growths have a center, the Marimo does not; it is simply algae all the way through.

Before you get worried about adding algae to your tank, this algae is not capable of spreading and growing like normal algae does.

The growth of this algae is extremely slow, and it is not capable of spreading randomly to other parts of the tank. It can only grow in clumps and does not attach itself to other objects in the tank.

While it does not naturally attach itself to decorations or other parts of the tank, it is possible to glue the Marimo to various areas of the tank as decoration, though this can cause long term damage.

While it is possible to create extremely attractive "grassy" areas of the tank by gluing multiple Marimos to one area, or creating faux trees with them, it can cause them to rot.

Even though this algae, like most algae, is extremely hardy, it is prone to rot under certain circumstances. This rot is the main killer of Marimos in aquariums, and it is mostly caused by incorrect care or water parameters.

WHY DO THEY COST SO MUCH?

When you first go to buy a Marimo moss ball, you may find yourself surprised at the price. They are often $6-8 for just one moss ball, or $10 for three mini moss balls.

In the big picture, this isn't really that much. But for this price, you could get multiple java ferns, or multiple Anubias, or several large bunches of Brazilian water weed.

So why does this algae cost so much when compared to common aquarium plants?

The primary reason for the price is the slow growth of this algae.

While java ferns and Anubias also have slow growth rates, large production firms can increase the rates of growth with fertilizers, high lighting, and ideal water parameters.

However, fertilizers have little to no effect on the growth of a Marimo Moss ball.

These moss balls normally only grow one half to one centimeter per year. This is extremely slow growth, and since they are primarily propagated by asexual reproduction, it can take four or five years to grow them large enough to sell.

Due to the slow turnover rate, many are simply harvested from natural areas, which is also a costly expenditure.

Whether they are grown alongside other plants or harvested, it is very costly to grow them or produce new ones, resulting in higher costs.

MARIMO MOSS BALL CARE

Here are a few things you should know about caring for Marimo Moss Balls.

WATER PARAMETERS

In terms of temperature, these moss balls normally come from very cold water, but seem to do very well in any range normally seen in aquariums, though they can start to melt and rot if the temperature reaches over 80 degrees.

They can survive in a wide range of pH, but it seems like a more neutral or slightly acidic pH is best for them.

As far as lighting goes, they are not picky. Whether the lighting is low, medium or high, they will do well in the tank.

Water hardness also does not seem to play a large role in the overall health of a Marimo moss ball.

Their adaptability to nearly any type of water is one of the reasons that their popularity is rapidly growing.

CARE TIPS

Since Marimo Moss balls are neither plants nor animals, their care needs are a bit unique.

While most plants can simply be planted, fertilized, and forgotten about, the Marimo need slightly more intensive care.

It is recommended to roll your Marimo at least once a week. You can press it in your hand and roll it to keep a circular shape, or simply flip it every week in the aquarium.

They naturally roll around on oceanic floors, which helps them keep their shape.

Since they are not normally rolling around in aquariums, they can begin to develop abnormal shapes.

While the abnormal shape is not normally an issue, there is another issue that may arise – the bottom part of a Marimo will rot if it is not rolled frequently enough.

While they only need minimal exposure to light to live, the bottom part would not be exposed to light at all. If you wait too long to flip or roll your Marimo, you may find that the bottom part has begun to rot.

If the rot is not too bad and only some slightly discoloration, you can leave it on, as it may be able to recover.

On the other hand, if the rotten part has turned a deep or light gray, you should try to separate that section, roll it into a ball, and place it elsewhere in the tank.

If there are no signs of recovery after a few days, toss the rotten part to avoid an ammonia spike.

HOW TO CLEAN YOUR MOSS BALL

As they roll around, or as the water current brings particulates over to them, Moss balls tend to accumulate mulm and crud, similar to a sponge filter.

While a sponge filter cannot do anything with the mulm, Marimo Moss balls can use some of it. However, they often take in quite a lot more than they need and should be cleaned every few weeks.

To clean a moss ball, simply take it out of the tank and place it into a separate container of dechlorinated water.

Squeeze it multiple times in the water, and you should see mulm coming out of it. After squeezing it, you can reshape and place it back into the tank.

Note that after squeezing it, most of the water is also squeezed out of the Marimo.

This can cause it to float for several minutes to several days, which normally is not an issue. As long as it is able to sink again after 2-3 days, no problems will arise.

QUICK REVIVAL

Every now and then a Marimo will seem sick for no reason.

Your water quality may be absolutely perfect for them, everything else in the tank is thriving, your plants are growing quickly, but the Marimo is just sadly sitting in the corner, slowly turning brown or gray.

Even with frequent rolling, reshaping, cleaning, and good lighting, it just seems to rot away.

Even though Marimo moss balls are able to survive most water temperatures, they can occasionally become sick in water temperatures over 70 degrees, though this is uncommon.

To fix this problem, take your Marimo out of the tank and place it in a jar or other container of tank water.

Next, place it in your fridge overnight. Take it out in the morning and place it in or near a window.

Leave it in a cooler area, or just room temperature, where it is able to receive direct sunlight. After just one or two days, there is normally a significant increase in the health of the Marimo.

COMMON USES OF MARIMO MOSS BALLS

Marimo moss balls are commonly sold as "betta buddies", "tank enhancers", and "shrimp buddies". So, what are they normally used for?

For the most part, these algae balls are just decoration. They grow incredibly slowly, so they do not change much, and can be used as simple decoration.

While they will convert some nitrates into energy, it will not be enough to make any difference on the overall nitrate levels.

Some bettas seem to enjoy having them around, often resting on or near them, or even pushing them around the tank.

Shrimp absolutely love these moss balls and will sit on them for hours, picking at the mulm they collected. For shrimp, these moss balls are a feast.

Marimo moss balls can also be used in the creation of "Bonsai trees" with quite amazing results!

TANK MATES

When it comes to tank mates, most fish and invertebrates are perfectly safe to keep with the moss balls. However, some fish will develop a taste for them, and then you're out the money you spent.

For example, while a carnivorous fish like a betta won't eat them, a massive herbivorous fish like a goldfish will devour one in just a few minutes.

It is recommended to keep at least one Marimo Moss ball with shrimp due to the amount of biofilm that grows on the moss ball. Much of a shrimp's diet is biofilm, so having a constant source is always beneficial to their growth and health.

Since moss balls cannot possibly cause harm to fish or other creatures, the only restriction on tankmates has to do with the safety of the moss ball.

PROS AND CONS OF MARIMO MOSS BALLS

Here are a few common benefits and drawbacks of owning Marimo Moss Balls.

BENEFITS

Even though Moss Balls primarily act as a form of decoration, they have the benefits of normal decorations as well as other benefits that normal decorations lack.

Just like any other decoration, fish within a certain size limit are able to hide behind or among Moss balls, which will help them feel more secure.

They can also increase the overall aesthetics of the tank, especially if the tank has a natural theme. You can even cut them up and glue them to various areas of the tank, creating "moss" walls, "grass", and even "trees".

However, if the bottom part of the Marimo doesn't get any sunlight, it will rot.

They also help reduce nitrates in the aquarium, though not to an extent that would impact the frequency of water changes.

They will be taking out a very small portion of the nitrates, ammonia, and nitrite available, which can be beneficial in the long run.

As previously mentioned, they do need to be cleaned. However, this makes normal tank maintenance easier in a way.

They collect a great deal of mulm and hold it until you can clean them, which can lessen the amount of time you have to spend spot cleaning your tank.

Last but not least, they promote the development of biofilm and microorganisms. While this may not impact a tank that only has large fish, it is incredibly beneficial to shrimp, fish fry, and small fish varieties.

Some of them are able to eat the microorganisms as well as the biofilm that the Marimo grows.

NEGATIVES

The only negative that can arise from a Marimo Moss ball is caused by improper care. Since they are generally large and dense, if they were to rot and die, it could cause a severe ammonia and nitrite spike.

Ammonia and nitrite are leading killers of pet fish, and no fish is immune to them.

If you see signs of rot on yours, be sure that you are cleaning it every few weeks and rolling it once a week. Ensure that the water temperature is not too high, and if there are seemingly no causes, use the fridge method for a few days to try and revive it.

You can also remove the rotted areas and place them in a cup or bowl by a window, which may help revive that part. If not, at least it didn't release ammonia in the main tank.

SIGNS THAT YOUR MOSS BALL IS DYING

Since the death of your Moss Ball can have a significant impact on the overall health of your tank, be sure that you know how to identify early signs of death.

Keep in mind that the natural lifespan of this algae ball may very well be over 100 years, and due to their hardy nature, most can come back from significant damage.

The earliest sign is normally discoloration; not necessarily changing colors, but if some areas start to become lighter than others, there is a chance that your moss ball is dying.

If the Marimo begins to turn brown, yellow, or gray, it is a sure sign that your moss ball is dying. However, if this area is one that does not often see light, it is simply dying due to a lack of sunlight.

This algae makes its own food through photosynthesis, which requires an input of light and nutrients (waste). If it is unable to get the light it needs to make food, part of it will begin to rot and die.

However, if this part was already receiving light, there is likely something wrong with the chemistry of your water that is causing the issue.

Even though they do not directly require fertilizer, they still need to be able to access certain minerals found in normal tap water.

Of course, their tap water should be dechlorinated, as the chlorine can damage them and any other inhabitants you may have with them.

Try increasing the frequency and amount of water changes you are doing. This removes water that has more depleted minerals and replaces it with fresher water.

Normal tap water has enough minerals for this algae to survive, but it must be changed weekly to ensure the Marimo is receiving the proper amount of minerals.

HOW TO PROPAGATE YOUR MOSS BALL

Since some consider them expensive, wouldn't it be great if you could propagate your own moss balls?

Propagation normally refers to breeding animals or plants, but the Marimo moss ball is capable of asexual reproduction.

While they will not reproduce on their own in an aquarium, it is possible for you to propagate them. All you have to do is divide them into one or more smaller pieces.

Roll the smaller pieces and try to keep them as compact as possible, and place them back into the same aquarium, or into separate ones.

Over time, these will all grow and develop into separate little spheres. While they will often grow lopsided at first, reshaping them multiple times will help them grow into perfect spheres.

Since they grow so slowly, the growth will be more noticeable in smaller Marimo Moss balls than larger ones.

SIZE

Now, you may be wondering how large these are capable of growing.

For most plants, the maximum size will determine what aquarium you need to place them in from the beginning, as it often only takes a few months for them to reach their maximum size.

However, moss balls can be moved gradually to larger tanks, or separated into smaller ones if they grow too large.

They are capable of growing up to a foot in diameter, which is quite impressive for this rare algae.

While this size is not common in aquariums, simply due to the amount of time it takes for them to grow this large, they naturally occur at this size.

In aquariums, five or six inches is normally considered a maximum size, though larger is not uncommon.

They are normally sold between ½ and 2 inches in size, though there is no particular size limit on when they should be sold.

If you buy one of the larger ones, feel free to separate it into smaller ones if desired.

All in all, their care is very simple; moss ball + water. If they begin to look frail or sickly, place them in the fridge overnight and in a lit window during the day.

You can also start to remove any rotting areas to prevent the rot from spreading, and the separated areas may even make new moss balls of their own.

Made in United States
North Haven, CT
04 January 2023